MW01228792

CHOOSING
LIFE *after rape*

CHOOSING
LIFE *after rape*

WHEN AN UNEXPECTED EVIL
COLLIDES WITH
AN UNEXPECTED GOOD

WRITTEN BY
KIM ELLIOT

GRP

Choosing Life After Rape
Copyright © 2023 by Kim Elliot.

All rights reserved. No portion of this book may be reproduced, stored in a retrieval system, or transmitted in any form or by any means— electronic, mechanical, photocopy, recording, scanning, or other— except for brief quotations, without the prior written permission of the publisher.

Published in Nashville, Tennessee, by God of the Romanitque Publications.

Special discounts are available on quantity purchases by corporations, associations, and others. Orders by US trade bookstores and wholesalers—for details, contact the publisher at grpnashville@gmail.com.

Unless otherwise indicated, all Scripture quotations are taken from The Amplified Bible, copyright © 1987.

All rights reserved.
ISBN-13: 9798861611251
First Edition: 2023

DEDICATIONS

This book is dedicated to my mom, Linda Cavanaugh. How incredible it is to type out your name after all these years and feel the reality of the sacrifice you made of your freedom for us while missing your presence at the same time.

To my dad, Jack Cavanaugh. Only Heaven will tell of the many resources you gave up, in the name of love, to make room for us every time we needed it.

To my brother, Nick Cavanaugh, extended family, and all of our friends in Decatur, Illinois, who loved us and helped both of us throughout our growing-up years.

To my husband, Gary Elliot, who never expected to be a step-dude in the second half of the game. God's great grace always abounds through you.

Most of all, to my "trophy daughter," Andee, whose love makes both of us cry when we think about it for more than three seconds. I treasure the fact that there has never been one single second of my life that I regretted choosing you to love as my own.

TABLE OF CONTENTS

FORWORD

Lifelong friend. First call for every major *high* or *low* moment. The one who champions you and prays you through both the best and toughest seasons. A true **confidant**, so much so that you cannot remember life before them, and *certainly* cannot fathom life without them. These friends don't come around often, and from what I gather - many people don't have them. Because the type of person who can be all of those things, is so rare. Like, 0.01% of the population rare.

How did I find my confidant? My lifelong friend? ...I'm so glad you asked. The author of this book, Kim Elliot, chose to bring her into this world and cultivate her into the woman whose friendship has grounded me for 15 years.

Kim and Andee's story is one I know well. My mom and Kim have been friends for over twenty years. If you do the math, you can tell it took Andee and I a while to warm up, but once we shared our first belly laugh - it was on. Infinite discussions of this story with Kim and Andee could not have prepared me for how paradigm shifting this book would be. I have read the entirety of this book three times over, each time in just one sitting - it's one you simply cannot put down. Every pass I have taken over these pages has left me with hot tears running down my face, and with a greater revelation and understanding of the Father's love for us.

Most of us have only looked at the matter of choosing life, let alone choosing life after rape, from our own personal convictions. This book will prohibit any reader from remaining one-dimensional in their perspective. Kim has penned and published many a line that has left me transformed by truth - but *none* such as this. Letting us inside her inner viewfinder, allowing us to see every angle at which she processed and every turn she made - one thing is clear: trusting **Jesus** is the way.

Samantha Schendel

Owner of The Studio Downtown, Decatur, IL | Best Friend to Andee

INTRODUCTION

The Ground Round restaurant was just north of a significant east-west city street where I lived. It divides the less desirable central part of the city from its more desirable area, the upper north side. An abundance of convenience stores, grocery marts, and a variety of little strip malls line the street to cater to every need before heading farther into that upper north side where home happened to be for me and my family.

Another Friday night found my girlfriends and I looking for another good time out on the town. We started with some appetizers and Long Island iced teas. Having more than twice the alcohol of most cocktails, those dangerous Long Island iced teas made Ground Round one of our favorite places to kick off the weekend. We talked a lot about the things we thought would make the world a better place. Our understanding of "the world" was limited to our neighborhoods, schools, and current job drama. We were a bunch of Midwest girls who had barely stretched their wings. However, that did not restrain us from spouting off passionate ideas on how we thought the world needed to improve itself. You could call it armchair commentary on the local nightly news.

This particular night, the topic of abortion came up. My four girlfriends were very fiery as they articulated their opinions. All of them favored a woman's right to abort her baby. Secretly, I was taken aback by how impassioned they were. No one seemed willing to pound out any other option. Until this discussion, I had no idea how outnumbered I was among my friends on this topic. I was tempted to quickly agree with them to avoid conflict – or even the embarrassment of standing alone – and just move on with the night. Unfortunately, I am one of those girls with a tell-all face; my thoughts frequently on display. Verbally, I could have agreed with them, but my face would have given me away and revealed my secret. The truth was that I did have a deep conviction in my soul that there was a right answer to this question. I decided to drop eye contact like a kid in school and hoped to be overlooked, thereby allowing the conversation topic to change. You guessed it! Just like in school, no such luck.

My sweet and whole-grain hippie friend, who left peace and daisies everywhere she went, held the most liberal views of us all and was the one who asked me directly what I thought about abortion. I felt heat fire up the back of my neck as I pulled out every ounce of courage I could muster. Ever so gently, I dared to share my opposing thought, "I believe abortion is wrong, and good things can come out of unwanted experiences." Hoping that was the end of the inquiry, their collective disbelief pushed a rebound challenge at me with the most unthinkable circumstance they could personally muster: "What if a black man raped you? Would you get an abortion then?"

I don't believe they were suggesting that skin color would have made the violation worse. This was the 90s and race wasn't the sensitive topic it had been thirty years previously. Instead, I think they were considering how the outcome of a mixed baby would have been harder to accept in some communities.

I was still a virgin at this point. My friend circle, however, was well-experienced in casual sex. I could barely imagine having sex with someone I loved – let alone forced intercourse by a stranger. All I could think was that, regardless of the skin color and how hard it would be to explain to others, it did not change the fact that there was a right answer. That baby would be innocent of any wrongdoing. Hypothetically, they thought they had presented me the most gruesome predicament they could imagine, but I could not get past the baby's innocence. I said, "I still would not abort, because there is always the option of adoption."

There I sat like a unicorn within my friend circle – that one girl who would not bend in their direction. Of course, I'm sure they doubted my resolve and thought I was standing my ground out of pride. After all, what young woman could overcome such violation and then live through the shame that pregnancy would create? Wouldn't the child be a daily reminder of the event? Truthfully, I did not know if I could be that kind of girl. I just knew I would *want* to be that kind of girl who would take the wrong thing and do the right thing with it.

Eerily, as if they had prophesied it, less than a year later, my virginity was raped from me by a black man. I was pregnant.

॰◦

I have written two books on God's ways in romantic love, one published and one on the way. Those writing experiences were restraint-free. This is the first book where I painstakingly consider every word I write. The subject of a woman choosing to carry a child she neither planned nor expected is a profoundly personal experience that is as delicate as it is volatile. So many avenues of experiences must be looked down before crossing the road of language so as not to trigger unnecessary pain. I have lived out my own experience, took pregnancy center calls from other women in crisis in the middle of the night, and shared my story in classrooms full of unexpectedly expectant mothers and in churches and banquet halls filled with men and women eager to learn how best to help. As I write, the faces of many women who were confronted with unexpected pregnancies come to mind – women I have known personally, women hiding in large audiences who have approached me after I shared my story, and even the friends who shared the Long Island iced teas that night. Some aborted because of seemingly impossible personal circumstances or health risks. Others had harrowing experiences parenting those little surprises. Still others chose adoption or foster care. Here is a strong truth: every choice in an unexpected pregnancy is a hard choice, and it is a choice that will last a lifetime.

This book is, first and foremost, for individuals who are surprised to learn about their own unexpected pregnancies. Secondly, it is for those who want a story like mine to share with others how the God of the Bible can work in these circumstances. As the debate continues to rage over abortion, the choice to defend life is repeatedly rebutted by the objection, "What about in the case of rape?" This book is my answer to that question.

Obviously, I cannot present answers to everyone's experiences or hypotheticals; I will, however, present to you the One Who is the Source of all life, wisdom, and power. He is the One Who never left me or disowned me throughout my heartbreaking pain, impossible decisions, gentle healing, enormous needs, and unexpected desire to choose life for my baby and myself. Our story is the "What about in the case of rape?" story.

Thank you for reading this book. Many nights, my mom and I talked and brainstormed ways to get in front of the next girl or her partner who were trying to make the right choice concerning her unexpected pregnancy. I pray this book is finally the means we were hoping to discover.

CHAPTER ONE

THE RIGHT THING

"Hello?" I answered. A young man on the other end of the phone call introduced himself as a local high school senior, the son of a friend. He had an assignment with which they both thought I could help. His mom had given me a heads-up that he would be reaching out, so I enthusiastically obliged his request. He had been given a social studies assignment to report on a socially-controversial subject. His subject of choice was abortion. He asked approximately three basic questions about my personal experience, then asked the one question that made me stop and think: "If you had to do it over again, would you make the same choice and why?"

I had been a single mom on a low income for over ten years at that point. Andee and I were back living with my dad for the second time, waiting for our next apartment to become available. It was worth the inconvenient wait to keep my daughter in one of our area's most-coveted public schools – the same school from which this young man was preparing to graduate.

His question caught me off guard for one fundamental reason: choosing life and choosing to parent had not exactly been an easy bed-of-roses experience. I could not push out some thoughtless bumper-sticker tagline that promised people everything would go *their way* when they chose life. I knew that everything would be okay, *and* I knew that everything would not be easy. True for all things concerning life on Earth, right?

By that time, I had accepted a few opportunities to share my story publicly. I had determined to tell the truth every time I spoke. I would not smooth over the fear, shame, and hopelessness I danced with while making my decision to do the right thing. I determined not to overlook the many faces in front of me that may have made other choices nor the hearts that were still fighting mind riots of regret, shame, and condemnation. I took a long pause before answering him.

Would I do it all over again? Absolutely! I experienced a multifaceted love through my choice for life that I could never regret despite the many steep challenges of single parenting. However, not everyone who chooses life chooses to parent. Would I have still chosen life if I had placed my baby for adoption or if my child had turned out to be challenging to care for or love? Again, a million what-if scenarios I cannot answer specifically, but I can answer definitely. I would do it all over again. In the end, in spite of all the questions about how things might turn out for us, I had an incredible inner peace knowing I would stand before the One Who defines what is right as a girl who made the right choice. This was my answer. The young interviewer's stalled response revealed that it was not the answer he expected.

So, Who is the One Who defines what is right?

∞

I grew up under Catholic influence. My father was born into a strong Irish Catholic family, with confession every Saturday and mass every Sunday. He met all the holy sacraments up to marriage. Sacraments in the Catholic faith are like spiritual doorways to further one's faith before God and to stay in His grace. Our family history included nuns and attempts at priesthood. However, my family was not stringently devoted to Catholic ways. We attended church on holidays. My brother and I went to Catholic schools and completed and practiced our age-appropriate sacraments there. We did not have a robust ritual commitment, but we learned a strong sense of what was right through that exposure.

I knew that I knew there was a God Who made the rules by which we should live. I knew lying was wrong. I knew that fighting with my little brother was wrong, because it made my mom mad, and God made a rule that I should honor her. The only way I knew to avoid being a lousy sister was to blame my little brother for the things I did to him. I mean, as long as it could not be proven I was the mean ol' instigator, I was not guilty, right? Of course, that worked on my mom, but when I went into the confessional, I knew God would not buy it. Most of my "sins" as a kid in Catholic school were fighting with my brother and making my parents angry. What a rap sheet! I mostly did the right thing when it worked to my benefit and made me look good. However, when doing the right thing was going to cost me, I looked for a way out.

As young adults we begin to learn the long-term benefits to doing the right thing even when it costs us something. Doing what my boss said – like getting to work on time – cost some personal satisfaction, but afforded the long-term benefit of keeping my job. Elementary stuff, I know, but that did not sweeten the cost. It hurt to get up five minutes earlier than I wanted EVERY SINGLE DAY. For as long as my husband and I have been married, he remains baffled as to why I set my alarm and hit the snooze button five times before I get up. It might be some hidden inner demand I have to be in control of the time that I had to give away as a 21-year-old working at the music store. Who knows?

I can't say the Catholic experience gave me a real sense of pleasing the God of the Bible with my life or my decisions. I did, however, have a real sense of pleasing myself, my friends and family, and people in authority. Rarely were my choices to do the right thing selfless decisions. They may have appeared selfless to others, but most of the time, I made the right decision to benefit myself later down the road. It is the rawest level of human nature to consider ourselves before others. I don't know about you but I never met a considerate crying baby who thought twice about letting her parents sleep through the night instead of screaming for a feeding.

As a young adult, I mostly called on the God of the church when I was in trouble. My prayer was simple: "God, help!" It seemed to work a number of times. However, while waiting for my home pregnancy test result in the bathroom stall of the employee restroom, I watched my call for help slowly materialize its denial. I was pregnant. My brain turned to the staticky, snowy reception of a retro TV.

When I found myself unexpectedly expecting, doing the right thing for *myself* was the only thing I could imagine. Where was the girl back at the Ground Round who wanted to think of herself as the kind of person who did the right thing? Like an animal caught in a trap, she was panicked and afraid. I did not want to get an abortion, *and* I did not want to be pregnant. Author, Frederica Mathewes-Green, related about women surprised by an unexpected pregnancy: "Like an animal caught in a trap, trying to gnaw off its own leg, a woman who seeks abortion is trying to escape a desperate situation by an act of violence and self-loss. Abortion is not a sign that women are free, but a sign that they are desperate (Published in The Evangelical Catholic, Feb 92)." I wanted to turn back time to when neither situation was a reality in my life. Like all my friends, I considered abortion to be the only option that had the power to erase it all -- the rape, the pregnancy, and, hopefully, the memories.

A few days later, I picked up the phone at work and called an abortion clinic on the state line about 150 miles west of my home. I made the appointment and hung up the phone, knowing I could never make enough money to keep it.

"God, help!"

CHAPTER TWO

LET'S TURN BACK THE TIME

I was easily given to fate, believed in destiny, and dreamed of experiencing a once-in-a-lifetime romance that most want to claim for themselves—you know, one full of "suddenlies" and unexplainable coincidences. I longed to meet that one person who defied all odds to have me as his own. I wish I could say I possessed an ironclad conviction of waiting to have sex for marriage, but at the very least, I did have a firm conviction of not having sex without love.

A lot of peer pressure existed around me to join in on the sex, drugs, and rock n' roll. As of today, I still can't shake the rock n' roll! My drug use was minimal, and romance was nearly non-existent. I met my best friend and partner in "party crimes" at a college frat beer bash. I broke curfew the night we met to help her chase her midnight crush down the city's main cruising street in hopes of just making eye contact with him. She couldn't believe I did that for her. We were friends, thick as thieves, for years until she married the one man who took her as his own and continues to love her until death parts them. We relentlessly ran the roads for live music, and one night, we got a wild hair to plan a trip to the King of Rock n' Roll's homestead, Elvis Presley's Graceland, in Memphis, Tennessee.

We were excited to get out of town for the long Easter weekend. I discovered that Memphis had an Easter Sunrise service planned that Sunday, and I quietly considered going. That ol' Catholic holiday tradition called! We found a hotel in downtown Memphis. After settling in, we freshened up to grab some drinks at the hotel bar. While I was busy researching all the tourist things we could pack into the weekend, my friend was busy flirting with the bartender. In recent months, my dearest friend, who had more experience with guys than I did, often expressed her frustration over me not joining the bandwagon called "it's just sex." She may have wanted to have me on the same page with her or she may have wanted affirming company in the guilt of it all.

Or it could have been that my self-loathing was getting too heavy for her, and in her mind, if I'd just "give it up," I might finally get over it.

I had witnessed enough relational drama to kill my interest in anything casual. And of all weekends, it was this one where I was coming into a sense of peace about my desire to wait for love. I had lived through enough years of what it felt like to be the one percent of my friend circle who was not having sex – the odd girl out, the still-a-virgin, the "no" girl. I did not see any relationship around me that I aspired to experience – too much drama, heartbreak, pain, sadness, disease, and anxiety. I was growing content to wait for destiny to line me up with love.

We hit Sun Studios, the Peabody ducks, Graceland, and Beale Street. It was a fantastic start! On our last night, we decided to get all dolled up, grab a glass of wine, and find some live blues music on Beale Street. We found a velvety blues restaurant and bar with a subfloor stage. It felt so authentic – one blues player owned the stage, and the place was packed. I felt significantly grown-up with a slight rock n' roll sophistication. This place was different from our usual kind of local hang.

The waiter came to take our order. We ordered some wine, allowing him to choose, because we had no idea what was considered good wine. My friend noticed him being especially interested in me. She had a radar for that stuff. She brought it to my attention, and I rolled my self-loathing eyes at her. She fired up in frustration again and told me to stop thinking so lowly of myself. She pointed out that I was clearly desirable to someone at that moment, and she pushed me to consider his interest and left it at that. Even if I had dared to push past my self-hating lies, I still had no compelling interest in him.

Though this was not the usual hang for us, it did have the usual results for us...we drank too much. Having grown friendly with the waiter on Beale, we invited him to meet us at our hotel bar when he got off work. My friend and I laughed and had the best time trying to walk back to the hotel. I'm sure onlookers did not share our drunken humor over our exaggerated swagger.

Once back at the hotel, we grabbed a table with some other guys who were visiting Memphis, too. We hit the dance floor and chatted off and on as the night continued. I was beginning to sober up when the waiter from Beale arrived and took a seat next to me. I was kind, and his interest in me grew more intrusive as the night progressed. He made a couple of advances that I pushed away. Why do women always feel pressured to continue being nice in the face of unwanted advances? I wish someone had told me how to say "no" before "no" would be too late. Before long, my best friend snuck off with the hotel bartender she had eyed the night we arrived. I got annoyed. After all, this weekend was about friends – not dudes – and I was not ready to retire for the night.

The waiter from Beale offered to take me to see a live band not far from his apartment. I said yes because of my weakness for live music and out of spite for my best friend's current "love" occupation. His advances did not stop, though I pushed away every one of them on the ride to the club. He took me to his apartment first, and I insisted that we continue to the live music gig as planned. By that point, he was aggravating me.

We walked down the street and up a flight of stairs to a small venue where the band was playing its last song. Rolling my eyes, I ordered my own drink and stewed for a minute at how crappy my last night in Memphis was turning out to be. I put down my drink as the waiter from Beale came up behind me, pushed it away, said he had already bought me a drink, and placed it in my hand. Oh, another point of "how I wish someone had told me." All my refusals seemed to have worked until this particular "drink" was pushed at me. Unknowing to me at the time, this one was laced, and every defense I had before the drink evaporated except for my voice – saying "no" too late.

That Easter morning, I was not attending the sunrise service I had quietly considered before coming to town. Instead, I was waking up in a strange bed, my tights torn, sore, and sick with an unbelievable headache. What had happened slowly caught up with me, and I wondered desperately how to get out of that room. How would I ever get back to my hotel? The waiter from Beale, acting like this was a typical, no-big-deal, fun-loving experience for him, called a cab. Staring past him, feeling emptied out like a dry cardboard box, I hoped I would not do one thing to encourage one more ounce of interest from him. Deep in my soul, I begged, "God, help!"

Sitting in the cab, I hoped I was heading in the correct direction for the hotel and struggled to keep my emotions intact. As I let myself into the hotel room, my best friend held the phone, getting ready to call the police. I told her what had happened. As I attempted to shower the violation of will and body off me, she packed us up as fast as she could. She must have driven 90 miles an hour all the way home as I pressed my pounding, hot head on the icy window, praying a new prayer, "God, don't let me hate men." Why? I don't know, except that I had heard once on Oprah that women who are raped can end up hating men.

Thirty days later, I stared at that positive pregnancy test and wished I could turn back time. What do you do when you want to be the kind of girl who does the right thing *and* wants to turn back time?

Tell Mom.

CHAPTER THREE

TELLING MOM

Outside of my best friend knowing the events of that fateful night, I was alone in my thoughts over the violation for weeks. I found myself easily startled throughout the day, because I was so distracted by the trauma of the preceding weeks – so much so that other people noticed something heavy was going on with me. I could not afford an abortion, and I did not know what else to do. The only person I could think of to help me sort this out was the last person I wanted to tell – Mom.

Our home was undergoing some changes. Mom had gotten involved in a church she loved, and she believed that she was to stop working and stay home to serve God in prayer. And she had begun to open our home to others who wanted to know Him, too. I cannot say how keen my dad was on this change, but I can say our home was becoming a very peaceful place unlike any other time before. I discovered later that one of the people my mom fervently prayed for was me. She was that mom who gently suggested I hang out with better friends, went into my room while I was gone and prayed over my rock posters, and invited me to church a lot – minus all the condemnation when I turned up my nose.

She had invited me to a mother-daughter event planned at her church. She was beside herself with excitement over it, and because I loved her so much, I agreed to attend days before I found myself pregnant. The week of this event, the weight of the rape, the pregnancy, and the abortion appointment was too much for me. I could not imagine my mom showing me off to all her friends in that church, knowing the shame I was about to bring to her. My parents always insisted we kids could tell them anything and not be afraid to do so, and that familiar invitation kept ringing in my head. I finally broke down the night before the event and told her everything.

I watched her absorb every bit of the shock, control her heartbreak, and process all the trauma without losing eye contact with me. There are many evil things parents hope and pray that their kids will never have to experience, and there I was, one of her two beloved kids, canceling that hope. With great strength, she held me as I cried and told me everything would be all right. She told me to go to bed and that she would tell my dad the next day.

When I came home from work the next day, my dad stood on the front step waiting for me with tears in his eyes. I was a little surprised at his emotion. Our relationship had its difficult moments, making the depth of his response touching. He waited for me to reach him, and he hugged me deeply. To this day, the pain I brought to my parents' hearts is the most difficult thing for me to revisit.

I did not love God at this point. Honestly, the only one who loved Him was my mom, and even she struggled with the right thing to do, because she did not want me to hurt any more than I already did. As we discussed the abortion appointment, it was my dad who said out loud, "We don't do that. Abortion is murder." Immediately, I thought there was no way I could carry this child, nor should I be expected to do so; after all, I was raped. At that moment, I heard something I was not expecting, I heard that I would not be alone in this decision. I experienced a peace beyond understanding for the first time since the incident. The relief was overwhelming. In an instant, I was freed to think about this impossible and unjust situation and the other people it impacted from a new perspective. I cannot describe how pivotal it was to have other people share the load alongside me. We had not made a decision, but whatever it would be, I was no longer alone in it.

Imagine three adults in a room assessing the damage of a recent crisis. One person wants to turn back time. One person wants the pain to stop. One person wants to fix it, so the other two realize their deepest desires. That was my dad. Actually, I just talked with him on the phone while writing that last chapter. When I relayed what I was up to, he was excited to hear this story was being written, and he spontaneously recalled his moment in our family history that changed everything. He said, "I don't know what came over me [as we discussed the abortion appointment]. I don't know why I said it. I just knew I could not let an abortion happen without me saying it was murder. I just had to say it. I wouldn't have been able to live with myself if I didn't say it."

Let's go back to wanting to be a girl who does the right thing. I left off with the question, "Who is the One Who defines what is right?" As mentioned earlier, I was influenced by the Catholic church to know that the God of the Bible is the Definer of what is right. Since then, I have read the Bible for myself, and I can say that the Uncreated Creator of this universe, God, is the One Who has defined morality and ethics and written them on our hearts, which is more commonly considered our conscience or that inner "knower" that distinguishes right from wrong. For instance, you know that you know when the cashier gives us too much change, it is wrong to keep it. The only way we feel better about keeping it is by making up reasons why we think we are right to do so. Unfortunately, the problem in that scenario is that we are making up excuses. Making up reasons to do wrong things makes ourselves our own gods. To be our own god is the beginning of bad endings.

I received some"God, help!" answers that I want to point out here.

First, Romans is a book in the Bible. When you look at the first chapter and read through verse 20, God tells us through the writer that all of humankind know God exists because of the nature surrounding us, and we instinctively (in our hearts) know right from wrong. He adds that humankind are without excuse for denying He exists and for choosing to do wrong things. Truth and discernment were put into our hearts as He put us together in our mothers' wombs. Another verse, in the book of Deuteronomy chapter 30, verse 15, reads like an open-book test concerning the abortion question. God is speaking to His kids who are in trouble, who cried out, "God, help!" He replies to them, "… I have set before you life and death, the blessings and the curses; therefore, *choose life*, that you and *your descendants* may live" (NKJV).

Don't be impressed that I know this! I did not know these scriptures when I was looking for a way out of my trouble. All I had was a God-given conscience like you, recognizing the truth when I heard it. Recognizing the truth is not the hard part. The hard part is following through with it. Once we recognize it, the personal cost comes screaming – begging you not to think twice: save yourself from the cost! We all do it: choose our own selves first in subtle and life-changing ways. That was me – not a lover of God – just another lover of my own life.

I knew what was right, and I knew it would cost me more than money. It would cost me my life as I knew it. My first instinct was to save myself from everything I feared: shame, embarrassment, the hurt my family would experience, judgments from others, and so much more. I just wanted the event to go away, and if there had not been a baby, I would have had the freedom to ruin my mental health by pretending it never happened. Pushing it down, pushing it away, and raising a wall to hide behind would have been my fate if there had not been a baby. Ultimately, choosing life gave me life, just as the Bible promised.

Secondly, bringing your trouble to God – even if all you know to say is, "God, help!" – is more than enough to get the ball rolling in the right direction. Not being alone in my decision was crucial in helping me consider other options that did not seem possible at first. If your "help" is not directing you to choose life, as we know to be right, visit a Christian crisis pregnancy center. They believe in the impossible, walk beside you on the journey, and lead you to the resources to accomplish what our "knowers" inform us is the correct path. Many of these centers will even arrange for you to see your baby through performing an ultrasound. The truth really does set us free (John 8:31-32). Each time I heard the truth, I was set free to think another thought, to feel other feelings.

Thirdly, instinctively knowing what is right and choosing to do it regardless of what it will cost us develops some deep-seated value that defies explanation. That choice raises our sense of significance as a person – like grabbing hold of some divine courage that empowers us to cross the "chicken line" to do the right thing. As I considered alternatives to abortion, I not only saw possibilities differently, I saw myself differently. My lungs filled up as strength grew in me. I became more of a champion than a victim of rape. I had the opportunity and the ability to be a girl, better yet, a young woman, who could do the right thing even though it would cost her. This baby was innocent, and I had a chance to champion someone else's existence even though I might never experience a personal benefit from the choice.

To my readers deciding what to do with their unexpected pregnancy, I encourage you to choose life. Regardless of how you got here, you are here. An innocent person is awaiting your help. You know what is right. You also know that it will cost your life as you've known it. At this point in my decision-making, I learned that telling others who loved me what had happened opened the door to more help than I first imagined. Those who also want to do the right thing will come alongside, and you will not be alone in all the steps that follow. I also learned that one open door does not lead to an instantaneous Hallmark ending. It leads to another open door. God, your Creator and the Creator of your baby, lights up our paths one step at a time. I know you want to know everything now – today – but He wants you to know Him. And over every threshold you dare to cross, you will.

My next door? Adoption.

CHAPTER FOUR

NOT A HALLMARK ENDING

Five months into the pregnancy, I learned that I was carrying a baby girl as I began to explore the adoption option. Secretly, I had wished the baby was a boy, as if the less the baby was like me, the easier it would be to say goodbye.

A tiny office on the west end of downtown was nestled between a tiny law firm and a tiny video game consolidation store. I entered the inconspicuous front door into a reception area furnished with four chairs positioned in front of the picture window and a desk that had seen better days. The sweet, elderly receptionist was caught off guard by my request. She disappeared to discuss my request with the director and returned to dig out a file from a drawer in the old desk. She handed over the file and advised me that they did not arrange for adoptions like agencies did. They did, however, keep a record of families who had expressed a desire to become adoptive parents to children in need. Inhaling a deep breath, I accepted the information.

When we are young, we are taught our phone numbers, addresses, and how to dial for emergency assistance. Learning how to contact a crisis pregnancy center never makes the list of life's emergencies. Our city's pregnancy center was sufficient for its size. Its discreet location and presentation did make it hard to find which, I realize now, may have been a deliberate act of respect for their clients.

That is not the case these days. Christian crisis pregnancy centers, thankfully, now advertise through myriad avenues – radio, TV, billboards, Facebook pages, etc. – to answer the life question. The people there greeted me warmly; their kindness made it hard to leave. Their resources were limited, but their hearts for unexpected moms were huge. These pregnancy centers have progressed remarkably, and the national networking and impressive resources in place now are exceptional.

I brought the file of prospective adoptive parents home. I crawled onto my bed and read all the letters aspiring parents wrote to unexpected moms considering adoption. Every proposal read like a happily-ever-after Hallmark movie script. They were THE ideal couple with THE ideal home, family, and income. They loved children, of course, and promised the best future. Some could not have children, and others wanted to add children to their existing families. Every good intention was presented, and every good outcome was anticipated. I was not excited. I was overwhelmed. As much as each couple tried to set themselves apart, they all sounded the same to me.

How is one to decide? For me, every proposal read as too good to be true. Life is not a Hallmark movie. Even a Hallmark tragedy is too clean and predictable to be true. I began by pulling out the letters from families that looked most like mine. After a couple of phone calls, I learned my situation held an unexpected challenge. After all, everyone claimed to love kids and sincerely longed to be parents. I had a baby to share. What could possibly make a loving pre-parent decline such a generous offer? I was astounded to learn, shortly into the search, that a biracial baby was a deal-breaker for most. The rape was a deal-breaker for a few others. Was I talking with Christians claiming the parental love of Christ – except in the case of skin color and cases of rape? Unbelievable! My selection quickly narrowed to only two couples. One already had children, and the other couple had none. I felt the least I could do for this little one was to make sure she was somebody's first baby, like she was my first baby.

Handing over the baby that nested in me for nine months – even to loving, willing parents – was beautiful but unnatural. Biologically, everything in a woman's body transforms into that of a mother. No matter how necessary or selfless the choice, it was just not a natural choice. Amid this decision-making, I found my soul needing help. My parents' support was invaluable. The pregnancy center provided strategic information and resources. However, my soul was distressed from doing the right thing. This baby was a life I would let go into the hands of people I met through a letter and talked with on the phone. They seemed wonderful, like their letter, but they could not promise me a fairytale ending for my baby. Who could? The best of beginnings does not guarantee the best of endings.

Would my baby be okay if they divorced later? What if one or both of the parents met a premature death? Where would my baby go then? What if they had other children and they, knowingly or unknowingly, rejected my baby because of her skin color or how she was conceived? I felt the weight of the reality that my baby was a person who came with a lifetime I could not predict, protect or control. This innocent life, much like my own, would grow to need divine interventions at some point, too.

∾

Once we broke the news to friends, my mom shared my situation with her church. They could not wait to welcome me and my mess into their hearts. I began to attend church with my mom on Sundays. This large congregation would raise their hands while singing songs of praise to God. They worshiped Him like they personally knew Him. Growing up Catholic, I was accustomed to very short services with lots of structure. I never saw the enthusiasm for loving God like I did there. Slowly, I came to realize what my soul needed: Him. Before, I called on God only when I was in trouble, but now I was asking for His guidance and leadership. Clearly, with a growing belly, my life was no longer my own. Choosing life was one thing; choosing her life for her was another. Lying on my bed one afternoon, deep in the frustration of who to choose as adoptive parents, I spontaneously cried out, "I just want to make sure she gets to know Jesus!" That cry seemed to tip off my mom as to who would be the better choice.

With her help, I chose the couple who said they knew Jesus like my mom did. They were sweetly sensitive to my sacrifice; they saw the depth of the selflessness with which they would be rewarded. They frequently sent me stories of others who honored open adoptions and wanted me to know they fully expected to have that kind of relationship with me. As much as they expressed their empathy for my sacrifice, it could not sink as deep as my soul needed to feel it. They came for a visit one weekend, and it was awkward. Sitting next to them in church that Sunday left me fighting off thoughts that they didn't care about my upcoming grief as much as they cared about the upcoming baby.

Only God could know this kind of giving of your only child for the sake of others.

∽

On Christmas Eve, I stood in church for a midnight service, singing Christmas songs and asking God if I could please have this baby now! I was nine days overdue, and my body ached everywhere. Two days later, I went in for a check-up, and the doctor decided that the day had arrived. He broke my water, and Mom ran off to get my suitcase and sneak in a chiropractic appointment, because she thought she would be stressed. Hello! Baby-pusher here!

By the 3 p.m. hour, Oprah popped up on the TV screen, and she was here. Not Oprah, my baby! I never fantasized about what it might be like to be her mom, so imagine my surprise at how connected and warm I felt when I held her. She looked like an angel with sweeping black hair flowing over her forehead. So sweet and tender. So innocent. Her new life really was worth choosing. I knew it was a healthy choice to see and hold her, and I soaked her in as much as possible. My family and best friend also took turns holding her, saying hello while preparing to say goodbye.

That evening, the adoptive parents arrived and held her for the first time. Tears flowed from their eyes as I bravely introduced her to them. They were overwhelmed by the gift of her life. They were so deeply grateful. I watched them. I couldn't determine exactly how I felt until the following day. The adoptive parents came into the hospital room to hold her as I ate breakfast. My smile was fake that morning. My scrambled eggs wouldn't go down, and suddenly, I lost my appetite. Grief had paralyzed my throat. I would have to say goodbye to my baby. She and I had experienced an exclusive relationship for nine months. As much as I had tried to defer emotional attachments towards her, I could not deny the reality of our relationship. She was *my* daughter. I decided I wanted the whole day to myself with her. This was it. This was all the alone time I would ever get, twenty-four hours.

Tomorrow, I would say goodbye for who knew how long, if not forever. This was not the Hallmark ending I had anticipated.

CHAPTER FIVE

SHE'S STILL YOURS

My mom let me out at the front doors of the drugstore to shop for a few personal items on my way home from the hospital. I brought my purchases to the register, and the cashier, full of sunshine and rainbows, asked how my day was going. My mind raced back over the last nine months, retracing every tear and fear as I pushed to politely reply, "Fine." When she finished my sale, I looked at her, thinking, "You have no idea the depth of the sacrifice I just completed." At that moment, it was obvious that my life, even the doldrum exercise of drugstore shopping, would never be the same. I was someone different. I was brave, selfless, and awakened to a new depth of soul within me. I was someone's mom; the cashier would not have known it by looking at me.

My house was profoundly quiet that day. I went to my room to rest my post-labored body and mind. I did not fully understand what I had done. I knew it was the right thing to do. The adoptive parents knew it was an undeservedly generous thing to do. However, my mom knew what I had done. How could she not? She was a mom. She knew the cost upfront would continue to make withdrawals from my heart as the days and years marched on. She kept it to herself that day and, instead, went to bed, sharing her aching desire in prayer, "God, I just want to go get that baby." Surprisingly, she heard His reply, "She is still yours." He was right. In our state at that time, birth parents had 72 hours to reconsider their decision, and adoptive parents were not allowed to leave the state until that time expired.

After spending the night praying, she entered my room, where I had spent the night staring at the ceiling, not knowing what I was supposed to be thinking or feeling. She said, "Kim, if you decide to change your mind and keep your baby, I will remain at home and watch her while you work." Another door opened that I had never considered before. Another thought I had never thought before. My dad's voice canceled the abortion thoughts, and my mom's voice canceled the childless thoughts. Again, bringing to light the fact that I would not be alone if I made a different choice.

There was so much to consider! We brought the idea to my dad. He was torn between the compassion he felt for the adoptive parents and his own heart to have a granddaughter. He dared to say it was my decision to make, and if I chose to parent, I could continue to live with them as needed. What about a nursery? Two weeks earlier, my brother had moved out. Coincidence? No, Providence. What about a crib? Whose parents store their child's baby bed in their garage for 26 years? Mine! I was a responsible, young adult with a good job and good parents. What about my ability to parent alone? I called a friend who was single–parenting two-year-old twin boys. Does it get any more challenging than that? She told me every difficult detail about single parenting, yet nothing she said convinced me to say no for another moment. I called the lawyer, who called the adoptive parents. Then, I called my best friend to help me shop for the necessities at Walmart on our way to pick up my baby.

As I write, I can hear the voices of good-hearted people cheering, booing, and sighing with hopelessness. Unplanned pregnancies come from all shapes and sizes of circumstances. Adoption is right, beautiful, and Biblical. It is advisable in many circumstances – and never easy. Birth mothers, like single mothers, are heroines who hurt for all the right reasons. Women who abort are mothers, too, hurting for many more reasons. Two things they all wish: they had better circumstances and that they were not left alone in them. The Bible gives the ultimate advice when it comes to making decisions: let the peace of God be your umpire (Colossians 3:15, AMPC). I was guilty of not having peace about my adoption choice. I am grateful that so many do. Adoption creates families, and that warms my heart, but my adoption plan was not marked by the peace of God.

I knew the adoptive parents would grieve, because I changed my mind. It took courage to look them in their tear-filled eyes and let them know that my decision was not about them. It was about me; my lack of peace with the situation. The outcome was not unfolding the way any of us had expected. No one can comprehend the pain of the adoptive parents' loss like another adoptive parent who experienced the same, and no one can know the pain of the birth mother's loss like another birth mother; these losses are simply sacred and to be honored.

Childlessness is painful – whether a woman chooses it or it chooses her. During my third month, lying on my belly in bed one night, I felt the tickle of what I imagined to be a butterfly in my abdomen. I thought it odd until I remembered, "Oh yeah, I'm pregnant." It was still unbelievable to me. I was feeling my baby. Such incredible wonder struck my heart as I wrestled with deciding whether I had permission to enjoy it. I wished the rape had never occurred, and now I was carrying a baby, planning to give it away. If I enjoyed the pregnancy in any way, I might love the baby, which would make this extra hard, right? I could not shake the wonder of it all and went to the library that week to check out a couple of books on pregnancy and birth, along with a video by Nova called *The Miracle of Life*.

Watching that video changed my entire perspective on choosing life. The documentary contained actual footage of the reproductive activity that may or may not produce a new life. I was unaware of the nearly impossible specifics that needed to align to create a human life. So impossible that it could only be orchestrated by an Intelligent Designer, the God of the Bible. Men and women do not have sex and just accidentally get pregnant. Men and women have sex all the time to make babies and cannot get pregnant. They move on to spend a lot of money and still do not experience a 100% procreation rate. God is involved whether we like it or not, whether we choose to believe it or not. Mankind does not create offspring; they procreate, meaning they work with the Creator on this pre-designed baby-making gig. According to the book of Psalms in the Bible, chapter 139, verse 16, all the days a baby is formed and will live are written in God's book before one of them takes place. In other words, before that baby surprised you, before you began to make decisions for them, God had already written out the days of their life. Isn't that incredible? Before you knew you had a baby coming, God was already at work forming that child inside of you.

The most compelling revelation I received from my learning was that I did not have to get pregnant, but I did. I was raped. I was a virgin. Was this child the consequence of rape or the reward of choosing life? The answer is yes. She was and is the rewarding consequence of experiencing a wrong thing and choosing the right thing. I determined I would not be ashamed, and I would follow through with dignity. I began to feel God's pleasure – not only in my choice, but in my attitude.

∽

I clearly remember looking my best friend in the eyes as we rode the elevator up to the hotel room where the adoptive parents stayed. I was nervous, but she was about to come out of her skin, anticipating their reception of us. She devised an action plan, "You get the baby, and I'll get all the stuff." She was comical, acting as though we were kidnapping my own child. It was a very somber and humbling experience, for them and for us, because we were all sympathetic to one another's pain. Nothing they could say would change my mind, and nothing we could say would ease their raw grief.

We got in the car to go home. We had been so eager to get that painful conversation behind us that we had forgotten to buy a car seat for the trip home. I held my daughter in my arms for her first ride home. When we arrived, my dad waited on the doorstep – the same doorstep where I found him crying over the discovery of this pregnancy. He now grinned ear-to-ear to be her grandpa after all. He and my mom had set up the crib and modified full-size sheets for immediate accommodation. My dad and my best friend went in search of a rocking chair, and I was left alone with my new baby, Andee. I laid her down to nap for the first time in what had been my first crib. Alone in the house, standing in the kitchen minutes later, I heard the most bizarre sound that I could not identify – a soft, whimpering cry. Looking around the room, puzzled by that weird sound, it dawned on me that my baby was calling for her mom! I was a mom, and suddenly loving her was the most natural experience that has yet to find its end.

CHAPTER SIX

THE SECRET SAUCE

This may be the part of the story where you would expect me to declare how we both lived happily ever after. Nope. From the beginning, I promised to keep it real. I'm not much for fluff and misrepresenting what a happily-ever-after really is. We are still living out this story.

My beautiful daughter is now a grown, God-loving woman who married the boy next door. They are raising two equally beautiful boys whom my husband and I affectionately refer to as "The Tornadoes," while we not-so-secretly hope for more. We live ten minutes apart. We enjoy an endearingly close relationship and always have. That does not mean life was easy for the two of us. We lost my mom to cancer when Andee was only five. My dad underwent a short stay in the hospital to overcome a lifelong struggle with alcoholism when Andee was in junior high. Money was always scarce. We moved a lot to make ends meet, and we were only able to enjoy two little vacations in 18 years. When she was in college, I suffered two pulmonary embolisms (near-death emergencies) with no insurance coverage. We were never the worse for wear, as the saying goes. We rebounded into more love and life every time. Even when provisions were tight, and in spite of experiencing much lack along the way, we were never without what we needed.

Most of the time, we thought we had better ideas of what we needed in our single-parent family. For example, shortly after Andee was born, my mom prayed that God would bring me a husband. God told her that there would be a man who hears His voice. That man did not come into our lives until *after* Andee herself had married. Once upon a time, I had been a girl holding out for a destined love, and I got it after all, but it was later and not through fate. It came through faith. It became a love story for the generations (and a book of its own). When God made that promise, that was not exactly the long-range plan I imagined as a single mom, but I was no longer in charge of my own life.

∾

Choosing to parent as a single was a good choice for me; God used my choice for life to save my life and to heal my heart, which had been shattered 400 miles back in Memphis, Tennessee. Choosing to parent positioned me to cling to a Man. A Man I would later learn had been waiting in the background of my life for a long time. Waiting to love me as His very own. He was the only Man around Who *wanted* to take responsibility for the two of us. He never thought about what it might cost Him to love the likes of us. This Man brought us both into His heart and His family, healed my brokenness, restored my losses, provided for our home, and made us believe we were worth love. If that weren't enough, He also encouraged us to dream with Him in the face of so many impossibilities. We are still together! And His name is Jesus. He considered us worthy of His unending love and attention, and I gave Him full charge of my life. Therefore, it was and is no longer my own.

Everyone with an unexpected pregnancy has their own story of how it came to be and is, also, very likely plagued with some level of regret. We either made a poor choice that resulted in an unplanned pregnancy or something was done against us. Both situations will require forgiveness. Forgiveness is pardoning an offense and releasing feelings of resentment toward someone. In my case, I needed to release forgiveness to the waiter from Beale Street, a man I barely knew – the man who raped me and stole my virginity. I had no idea how to do this until God gave me more understanding; I needed to experience forgiveness for myself first in order to release it to another.

"Forgiveness for what?" you may ask. Forgiveness for *my* sins, every single one of them. Sin is simply to miss the mark of doing what is right in God's sight. One of the initial things I learned about God's forgiveness was that everyone is born with a nature to live for themselves, which is rebellious towards a God Who is Holy. The more I learned about God and His desires, the more I saw I had hurt Him a lot throughout my life. Worse yet, I could not find the "secret sauce" to stop hurting Him – sinning against Him. That's when I learned about the gift of salvation. I learned that every hurtful thing I did to others and to God Himself required me to pay a debt to be in good standing with Him, which sounded scary until I heard the rest of His story. The debt I owed was already paid in full by Jesus. He was completely innocent of any wrongdoing, yet He said He would pay for my wrongdoings, so I could be one with Him and the Father. I was pardoned of a million wrongs even though I did not deserve it. Jesus was pure and did not deserve my punishment, but love compelled Him – a love I could not comprehend.

Being forgiven was the beginning of my experience with Christ. Not only was I forgiven of all my sins – past, present, and future -- He made me a new creation. He gave me a new nature empowered by His Spirit to change, be brave, and go and sin no more! Now, understand, I am still learning to live through His Spirit for all its worth. Sin happens, but it is no longer who I am. I live forgiven.

As I was learning how to love my baby, I was also learning how to be loved by Christ. So many times, I was flooded with love for my daughter, and God's Spirit would let me know His love for me was just like that – only better and more pure. As I grew in my understanding and experience of this reality of love and forgiveness, I was empowered to forgive the man who raped me, release my resentments, and ask God to forgive him, too, because, after all he too was a sinner like me.

Not one second of one day have I ever looked at my daughter and saw a violation. I have only seen a joy I did not deserve. She also has no problem letting others know she is my "trophy daughter" for choosing life. She never went without her needs being met. Often, her wants were granted through others I could never repay. I remember a time that she wanted to play the flute in grade school. I knew that there was NO WAY we could afford a flute, especially one that might end up in the closet the following year. Lo and behold, she came home with a beautiful flute as a gift from a friend. I didn't even get a chance to pray about it; God had her all to Himself that time. At school she showed no lack of self-confidence or being well-love, she was perfectly-adjusted, according to her teachers. As much as I thought I needed a husband to be her father as she grew up, God connected us with families whose father was the exact temperament and voice of wisdom she needed at different times in her life. God fit everything into a plan for our good, but not the kind of "good" we always expected.

God's definition of good was not the same as my definition in the beginning. My idea of good was getting everything *I thought* was good for us: money, a white-picket-fenced house of our own, cute dogs, a job I liked, a husband and dad in the home, and so much more. However, God's goodness turned out to be one of the most unexpected experiences of all – and probably the most difficult lesson I have learned in coming to know Him and His ways.

In the book of Romans chapter 8, verse 28, the Bible promises, "And we know that God causes everything to work together for the good of those who love God and are called according to his purpose for them..." (NLT). I believed His goodness was all about my comfort and happiness, and I kept waiting through all the challenges for the good part. You know, the feel-good part where I would win the lotto, be set for life, and everything would come my way. I experienced several years of frustration before someone led me to the next verse, which thoroughly defined what "good" God is working: "For whom He foreknew (to choose Him) He also foreordained (planned) to be conformed to the image of His Son..." (Romans 8:29 ASV). God's definition of good is the outcome of us becoming more like Jesus in our nature, desires, and actions. Understanding that the whole point of life was for a good and Holy God to take everything and to fit it into a plan to make me more and more like His Son (not necessarily comfortable for the sake of it) helped me understand that my life had great worth to Him. I never again wanted to cheat Him out of an opportunity for my good. From that day forward, I no longer wanted to be in charge of my life, and daily surrender came much more easily.

∽

For my readers who have experienced or are experiencing an unplanned pregnancy and need to forgive or be forgiven, an authentic experience of release, cleanliness, peace, and hope await you inside a relationship with Christ Jesus. He will make you a new creation. You will stand before the perfect and Holy Father of all creation as one "justified," meaning "just as if you never sinned!" It's true! That is the purifying power of the blood of Christ's sacrifice for you. He is the only innocent man able to meet the requirements of God to bring you home with Him once and for all time. The only thing you must do is to believe Christ made the payment for every single one of your wrongdoings – past, present, and future – by dying on the cross as though your sin was His own and rising from the dead to live again – this time, in you. That's it! Tell Him you believe it, and His promised Holy Spirit will move in and make you a brand new person who loves Him. It will take time for your mind to catch up with the new you, but that's where "fitting everything into a plan for your good" comes into play! He will be standing in you, working your past and present into a future of knowing Him, becoming like Him, and making Him known.

He will provide you with everything you need and many things you want. Remember the husband I thought I needed in the beginning? He slowly became less of a thing I *needed* and more of a thing I wanted. Christ became my greatest companion in the waiting, and He gave us both an enchanting love story with Himself at the center of it all.

He will also – hang on for this one! – give you the will and the ability to forgive those who violated you. It takes time to work through your thoughts and feelings until forgiveness has its healing effect in you. Jesus will be with you, and in you, to accomplish this work. Through salvation, He gives you Himself, the Forgiver of all sinners, moves in and shares with you what only He can: undeserved forgiveness for those who have hurt you. **Even the forgiveness you may need to forgive yourself.** It is His forgiveness He is giving. Be patient with this process and yourself. Take every thought captive to Him and openly tell Him what you think and feel. Let Him share in your grief and tell you what He thinks and feels about the same situations. My mom used to assure me that forgiving someone does not mean that they were ever right in what they did. As you stick with Jesus on this journey, He will bring you out to freedom, and He will walk with you and work in you to help you become more like Him along the way. He is the "why" that now empowers you to do the right things moving forward.

Choosing life for your baby can be more than a choice of letting your baby live. It is choosing LIFE Himself, Christ Jesus, Who says He is The Way, The Truth, and The LIFE. Jesus is LIFE. He is the LIFE waiting to be lived in and through you, the only Forever Companion you will ever have. The LIFE He has waiting to bring you is abundant and never-ending. It is nourishing, satisfying, and sustaining like bread. Your life will never be the same when you choose LIFE with Him. He is our "happily-ever-after"!

CHAPTER SEVEN

WHERE WAS GOD

Looking back, I now see I was never alone in my decisions. Even though I did not love God as my own initially, He was next to me, guiding me to my choices. When I considered whether to abort or not to abort, He impressed my father to tell me the truth. My father's words resonated with the moral compass God created in me, and I chose His choice. When I arranged to have my daughter adopted, He did not give me the peace my conscience needed, and He even told my mom in prayer that Andee was still mine. I chose His choice. As I navigated so many different decisions to do the right thing for my baby and myself, He made His love known to me. He never abandoned or disowned me.

For the women and men caught in an unexpected pregnancy, I invite you to read Psalm 139 in the Bible. As if gazing into a mirror, see yourself in it as you read. God is intimately acquainted with you. He is the One Who knows you best; after all, He wrote out all your days – even today, the day you would be reading this book. He saw your own conception and formed you from *His* desire to love you whether your parents wanted you or not. He created a space within you where He could move in and live in you as one. He will be there to help you do what you think you cannot. Every hard and painful day was written down in His book. Those are days He wants you to invite Him to take the lead and make all things possible through His love and power. Today is another invitation, because His mercies are new every morning. Discover how God has known you from the foundations of the Earth and designed plans to redeem every bad day. Let Him love you through every word.

Psalm 139 says…

"Lord, you know everything there is to know about me. You perceive every movement of my heart and soul, and you understand my every thought before it even enters my mind. You are so intimately aware of me, Lord. You read my heart like an

open book, and you know all the words I'm about to speak before I even start a sentence!

You know every step I will take before my journey even begins. You've gone into my future to prepare the way, and in kindness, you follow behind me to spare me from the harm of my past. You have laid your hand on me! This is just too wonderful, deep, and incomprehensible! Your understanding of me brings me wonder and strength. Where could I go from your Spirit? Where could I run and hide from your face? If I go up to heaven, you're there! If I go down to the realm of the dead, you're there too! If I fly with wings into the shining dawn, you're there! If I fly into the radiant sunset, you're there waiting!

Wherever I go, your hand will guide me; your strength will empower me. It's impossible to disappear from you or to ask the darkness to hide me, for your presence is everywhere, bringing light into my night. There is no such thing as darkness with you. The night, to you, is as bright as the day; there's no difference between the two. You formed my innermost being, shaping my delicate inside and my intricate outside, and wove them all together in my mother's womb. I thank you, God, for making me so mysteriously complex! Everything you do is marvelously breathtaking. It simply amazes me to think about it!

How thoroughly you know me, Lord! You even formed every bone in my body when you created me in the secret place; carefully, skillfully, you shaped me from nothing to something. You saw who you created me to be before I became me! Before I'd ever seen the light of day, the number of days you planned for me was already recorded in your book. Every single moment, you are thinking of me! How precious and wonderful to consider that you cherish me constantly in your every thought! O, God, your desires toward me are more than the grains of sand on every shore! When I awake each morning, you're still with me..." (The Passion Translation, TPT).

I invite you to pray: God, I welcome your searching gaze into my heart. Examine me through and through; find out everything hidden within me. Put me to the test and sift through all my anxious cares. See if there is any path of pain I'm walking on, and lead me back to your glorious, everlasting way – the path that brings me back to You.

Now, reread Psalm 139, and this time look through its lens and see your baby in it. Your baby was planned and designed by Him just as you were. With Him, you can choose the right future for you both.

Finally, for my beloved readers included in the one percent of unplanned pregnancy statistics with me – those who were raped – our harm was not God's plan, but our babies are. What our enemies meant for evil, God meant for good to save many lives (Genesis 50:20). Even though we may have experienced harm, God's plans will trump every abuse in ways you have yet to imagine. Let Him make something beautiful out of your bad experience. Better yet, let Him make *someone* beautiful out of your bad experience. That child is a rewarding consequence. Choosing the "right thing" is designed to heal you.

Everything will work out for good, *and* yes, everything may be difficult at the same time. But, with God, it will all be possible. Just start with: "God, help!"

AFTERWORD

Note from a "Trophy Daughter",

The choice for life is not easy. It's painstaking, exhausting, and complex. Certainly, we can add at least 20 more adjectives. But what resulted from my mom's choice for life is more than anyone could have imagined. I'm sure some people expected me to be a poor statistic and for my mom to be one, too! She was a wounded, young woman who could have ended up involved with a revolving door of men, which would have, in turn, messed up her kid too.

Imagine the hurt I could have felt, the boy trouble I was bound to get into, and the confidence-lacking woman I could have become. As a child born out of a negative situation, I have turned out to be blessed with the best life! I'm grateful to share with you what I have experienced, because all the odds were stacked against us from the start…but for God.

I was a fatherless black girl raised by a white mom. **But God**…

You can picture in your head the stereotypical outcomes of what a black girl without a dad can be, they are played out in our world daily. And yes, I know I'm not fully black, but the world sees me as black. Not mixed or bi-racial. I usually get the "light-skinned" assumption. God overruled the statistical forecasting and placed fathers in my life from the beginning and into my adult life, right up to the world's most amazing father-in-law and a very generous step-dude. God has made it for me to never feel fatherless. When I was younger, I was invited on daddy-daughter dates. I was bear-hugged regularly. I was accepted no matter what. I was carried to my mom's car when I fell asleep because a "hang-out" had gone too late. I was cared for, and my needs – and even some wants – were provided. I have never felt a gap because I did not have a father of my own. Those "shared fathers" have all loved me as their own in their own individual ways.

I should have scars. **But God**…

I actually wonder every once in a while, and more frequently now that I have a family of my own, if I have siblings or another set of living grandparents. I wonder about a whole side of my DNA that remains a mystery to me. Yet, I do not feel any ill will toward the man who violated the greatest woman on the face of the earth. Okay, I may be a little agitated that someone did that to my mom. But no anger. No resentment. And I pray he is doing well.

My confidence should not be great. **But God**…

I know my worth; I know who I am most days. I was taught young that I'm a daughter of the King, and that He loves me unconditionally. I am a mom of two phenomenal little boys now, and THAT IS A JOURNEY into learning more about who I was made to be, for sure. Ha! For the most part, I am a confident and competent woman. No one is ever 100% confident and competent, right? We all do things afraid sometimes. Should I have daddy issues? Nah, I don't. I'm cool with it.

I should have been wrapped up in boys and looking for love in all the wrong places. **But God**…

I was not a girl wrapped up in boys, sleeping around. "Boy drama" was exactly that – DRAMA! Throughout middle and high school, I watched the relationship drama my peers experienced. It was exhausting. No, thank you. I had crushes. I had moments of "I wonder why some of these dumb boys don't like me." So, instead of entertaining the drama my senior year, I ditched school a lot to hang out with my homeschooled best friend from church. She had a brother that I fell in love with, married, and had his babies. It was not a surprise to my mom. Well, I mean, the ditching school part was a surprise, but not the boy. She told me God woke her up in the middle of the night and told her I would find my love my senior year of high school. What a life! And yes, my high school BFF is still very much my BFF, despite her brother "stealing" me from her.

The outcome of my grandmother's, grandfather's, and mom's choice for life has produced SO much more than a life. It has produced a full life. I really wish my grandma was here to see and experience what her sacrificial "yes" has produced. Only by the grace of God did our story turn into what it has. He's too good of a Father to allow His children to experience a wrong and not plan to right it. And He will do the same for you and those for whom you care. I pray that whoever reads this story is filled with hope, courage to do the right thing, and a peace that transcends your understanding and current situation.

To my family and friends, who chose my life over their own, I will never have the words to thank you enough for allowing God to move in your hearts and through your

lives. It gave me a life to live, a life that I hope has honored God and each one of you in some way at some time.

Andee Miller

Wife | Mother | Trophy Daughter

2019, Beale Street, Memphis, TN

Andee, myself, and her first born to come
standing in front of the cafe where what was "…
meant for evil agianst me God meant it for good,
to bring it about that many people should be kept
alive, as they are today. So do not fear; I will
provide for you and your little ones."

Genesis 50:20-21 ESV

CARE-NET.org Decision Resources

Need immediate support with a pregnancy decision?

Call to speak with us about your options. We're available to talk M-F, 10 am - 5 pm EST. You can ask us anything; we are here for you. We can also connect you with a local pregnancy center in your community.

Phone: 877-791-5475

The mission of Care Net's Abortion Recovery and Care (ARC) program is to lead the way in abortion recovery through resources and programs that connect, equip, and support those seeking healing for themselves and/or providing for others.

Healing from the pain of abortion is a journey. Whether you had an abortion last week or 40 years ago, we're here to help.

Phone: (703) 770-8000

Honest storytelling captures this reality in deep and compelling ways- which is what led us to launch Adoption is Beautiful - a movement to ignite an honest conversation about adoption in the United States.

Visit:adoptionisbeautiful.org

Kim Elliot is the Co-Founder of God of the Romantic Presentations with her husband, Gary Elliot. Together, residing in Nashville, TN, they are passionate about seeing singles come to rest in God's design and providence concerning their desires for love and marriage. Kim's rape, unplanned pregnancy, and redemptive love story can not be told without pointing to God's greater story in her life: His salvation, companionship, and purpose. Visit **godoftheromantic.com** to learn more.

For speaking requests email: **contact@godoftheromantic.com**

Choosing Life After Rape special discounts are available on quantity purchases by corporations, associations, and others. Contact the publisher at **grpnashville@gmail.com**

Books by Kim and Gary Elliot are available at
godoftheromantic.com/books:

The God of the Romantique by Gary Elliot

Veiled Unto His Pleasure by Kim Elliot

Choosing Life After Rape by Kim Elliot

Coming in 2024:

Violets in the Snow by Gary & Kim Elliot

Made in the USA
Columbia, SC
07 March 2024

32677498R00050